Other People

OTHER PEOPLE

Daniel Brooks

Other People
first published 2022 by Scirocco Drama
An imprint of J. Gordon Shillingford Publishing Inc.

Scirocco Drama Editor: Glenda MacFarlane
Cover design by Doowah Design
Author photo by Bronwen Sharp.

Printed and bound in Canada on 100% post-consumer recycled paper.
We acknowledge the financial support of the Manitoba Arts Council and The Canada Council for the Arts for our publishing program.

Library and Archives Canada Cataloguing in Publication

Title: Other people / Daniel Brooks.
Names: Brooks, Daniel, 1958- author.
Identifiers: Canadiana 20220430160 | ISBN 9781990737169 (softcover)
Subjects: LCGFT: Drama.
Classification: LCC PS8553.R658 O84 2022 | DDC C812/.54—dc23

J. Gordon Shillingford Publishing
P.O. Box 86, RPO Corydon Avenue, Winnipeg, MB Canada R3M 3S3

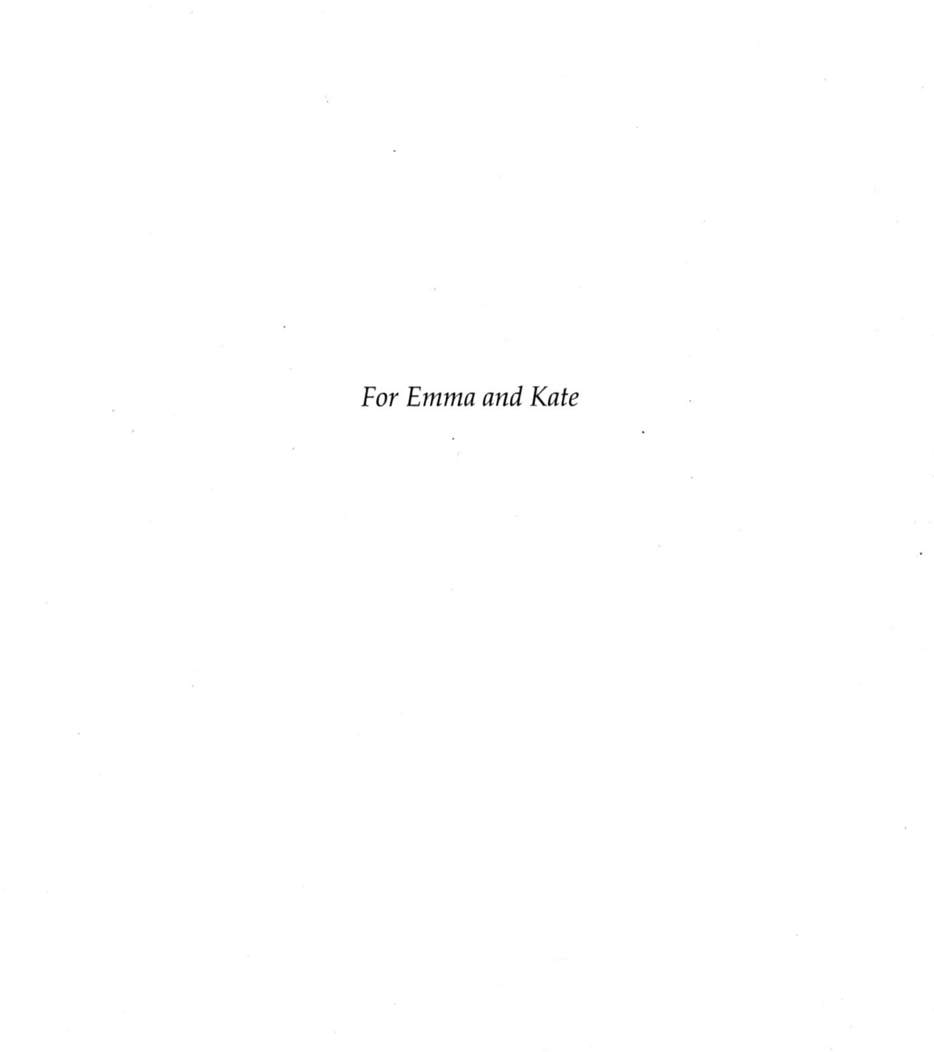

For Emma and Kate

Foreword

Brendan Healy

I'm 26 years old. I'm in the basement of a church on Dufferin Street in Toronto, rehearsing a play that I've written. I'm also directing and performing in it. The project is part of my studies at the National Theatre School. My mentor on the project is Daniel Brooks. I had never met him before this rehearsal. The folks at NTS had asked me who my dream mentor would be, and I said Daniel Brooks—never thinking that it would happen. And now here he is.

I feel nothing other than total embarrassment. Daniel watches me as I fumble my way through an unnecessarily personal piece, laden with the kind of angst that is perhaps to be expected from a 26-year-old theatre student. At a certain moment in the piece, I am supposed to break out into a dance to Public Enemy's "Fight the Power" that inspired Rosie Perez's iconic dance at the top of Spike Lee's *Do the Right Thing*. Looking back, this dance was perhaps a problematic choice on my part. But, in my defence, the moment was intended to make me look pathetic. I am not a dancer. I am nowhere close to being a dancer. And I am evidently a long way from Public Enemy's ethos, despite my love for them.

The cue begins and the song's harsh beat booms. Chuck D urges: *"Music hitting your heart 'cause I know you got soul."* It's time to dance. I ask myself: Can I actually do this in front of Daniel fucking Brooks?

I dance. I try to channel Perez's power and anger. At best, my dance is muscular. It is athletic. It is also awkward. It is silly. But it's cathartic. For me, at least. I feel fierce. I feel fully myself.

From the corner of my eye, I see Daniel. He, too, is dancing. And he is picking up some of my moves as he sweeps across the floor. I think: I like this guy.

***

Flash forward twenty years. I am sitting in rehearsal with Daniel again and, this time, it is he who is dancing in front of me. The music is from Stereolab and the context is *Other People*. I am too shy to dance as well.

The play's journey to me and to Canadian Stage began in the first summer of the pandemic. I receive an email from Daniel. Not Daniel Brooks. It's from Daniel MacIvor.

> *I'm writing to put you two together because Brooks has a good idea and I want to make sure he acts on it. He has some wonderful notions around a thing called The Perfect Human*

which sounds like a conversation with oneself about creativity and existence and cancer and mortality and suffering and joy. It feels like it could be a weekly thing, a podcast-y thing. I know you're open to new content, Brendan, and I was thinking you two might be able to work up something.

That's all.

Love to you both,

D

I respond. Brooks and I have a chat. There's talk of sharing some writing.

And then a year goes by with nothing.

It's the second summer of the pandemic when I receive a draft of what is now a play. I dive in.

The draft is dizzying; like being caught in a spiral.

As I make my way through it, I ask myself several times: didn't I just read this section? Gertrude Stein pops into my mind. Yes, Stein's desire to capture *process*: the mental process, the experience of consciousness, the infamous "continuous present." I wonder if this is the meditator's state of being.

I go back to reading the play.

It's not easy.

I reread the same paragraph three times while I think of Allen Ginsberg for some reason. Wasn't he a meditator? Or a Buddhist? Or both? I put the play down and pick up his *Collected Poems*. I love this piece of writing: *Well, while I'm here I'll do the work—and what's the work? To ease the pain of living. Everything else, drunken dumbshow.*

Get back to the play, Brendan.

***

I'm 33 years old. I'm sitting in a doctor's office at the cancer hospital (aka Princess Margaret) in Toronto. I recently had my left testicle removed because I found a bump and it has been confirmed that the growth was cancerous. Thankfully, though, it was caught early. The doctor has just told me that my scans are clear and that I won't be needing further treatment. The doctor leaves. I breathe a sigh of relief.

Before I can leave the tiny room, a volunteer must administer a survey to find out how satisfied I've been with my experience at the hospital. At that moment, cancer-free me is *very* fucking satisfied with his experience at the hospital. Suddenly, a nurse bursts into the room and orders the volunteer to exit. She informs me that the doctor had been looking at the wrong chart. She tells me that, in fact, my cancer has spread and that I'll be needing further treatment. She then tells me to wait for the doctor to return to get more details.

"Is it serious?" I ask.

"I think so," she replies.

She closes the door behind her.

I wait.

For forty-five excruciating minutes.

I'm no longer a cancer-free me.

When the doctor returns, the first thing he says is: "Well, isn't this a kick in the pants."

***

We never talk about cancer. As a society, I mean. We are so uncomfortable with public displays of dis-ease.

But then there is Daniel Brooks. Across the spectrum of works that Daniel has created, there is a rigorous commitment to revealing the *fullness* of the human experience. His observation and appreciation of the inner and outer details that give shape to our lives is, in part, what gives his theatre its vitality, complexity, and power. So, it is no surprise that Daniel is living his cancer with that same curiosity and dedication. It is the mark of a true artist.

As I make my way through the draft, I am often jolted by its naked humanity. It's humanity at its most comedic and tragic. My experience with cancer was completely dehumanizing. I was reduced to being a patient, a cancer victim. I became only my body—my sick body that needed to be cut, poked, touched, infused, tested, monitored, evaluated, invaded.

I continue to read the draft and I find myself crying—not out of pity for Brooks—but because the play returns to me something that cancer took away. Is this what dignity feels like? It's a difficult concept to understand until it is taken away. And when you feel it return, the concept becomes even clearer. Yes. That's what I love about Daniel's work. His art delivers dignity.

I reach the end of the draft and I am in love with it.

***

It's a few months after that doctor's visit. I am making my way through treatment. It's tough. I feel weak and depressed and alone. To make things more emotionally challenging, I'm also mourning the loss of my father who recently died from a brain tumor. Father / son cancer combo. At times, it's too much to handle and I am overcome with grief too heavy to carry.

I get a package in the mail. There is no return address. Inside is a book. No card. No note inscribed. Just a book. It's *Man's Search for Meaning* by Viktor Frankl.

My first reaction to this gift is to get pissed off, which is often the case when I'm confused. Why would someone send me a book from someone who survived *Auschwitz?!* And, then, not even tell me who they are? Is this some kind of joke?

I leave it on my desk. Months go by. I make it through my treatment. I am finally clear of cancer. It's cancer-free me again. But I'm not the same me that I was prior to cancer. That me is gone.

One day, I am cleaning off my desk and I pick up the book. I initially intend to leaf through it but I end up reading the whole thing right there. I am so moved by its message of hope, resilience, personal responsibility, inner freedom. Frankl's profound appreciation of beauty and art and nature speaks to me deeply. To my bones.

I regret not reading it when it landed in my mailbox. It was just what I needed.

Maybe I wasn't ready to receive it then.

I return to the question of who sent it to me. Immediately, I decide that it must have been Daniel Brooks. I just decide that it is him.

***

I think *Other People* has three stories. Or tracks. Or are they characters?

There is Daniel's body: a body dealing with age, dealing with cancer, dealing with the experience of ten days of endless meditation.

There is Daniel's mind. A great mind. A learned mind. A curious mind. A mind that is currently preoccupied with his mortality. A mind he is trying to overcome.

And there is Daniel's—oh gosh, can I say this?—spirit. I wish I had another word. The word "spirit" not as in "soul." But "spirit" as in that ineffable life force, that vitality, that *thing* that animates us. I see Daniel's spirit expressed in the other people in this play: his fellow meditators, his daughters, the mysterious "her" that eludes him, Robert Lepage, his best friend, his parents, and us—the audience—who are bearing witness to this event. They / we drive him, torture him, inspire him, push him, restrain him. And, as the practice of mettā-bhāvanā (the meditation of loving-kindness) in vipassana suggests, it is these other people (even you, dear reader) who ultimately provide him with a pathway to liberation.

Other people.

We witness them; they witness us. We define them; they define us. We create and destroy them. They create and destroy us.

I'm now 47 and I have yet to ask Daniel if he was the one who sent me Frankl's book. Maybe it's because I don't really want to know if it was him. Ever since I read the book, I've treated Daniel like he is the one who gave me that extraordinary gift. I like treating him that way. It makes him very special to me. And me special to him.

Toronto, June 2022

Brendan Healy is an award-winning theatre director, teacher, and cultural leader. He is currently the artistic director at Toronto's Canadian Stage.

Production History

Other People premiered at Canadian Stage in Toronto, Ontario, Canada, March 3–20, 2022.

Written and performed by Daniel Brooks

Directed by Brendan Healy

Dramaturge	Daniel MacIvor
Stage Manager	Arwen MacDonnell
Sound Design	Thomas Ryder Payne
Set and Lighting Design	Kimberly Purtell
Wardrobe	Ming Wong, Laura Delchiaro
Movement Coach	Adam Lazarus

The script was developed with the support of Why Not Theatre.

There is a chair, upstage right.

Music is playing.

A man enters. He places a glass of water near the stage. He dances. Closes door to theatre. Steps onto the raised stage. He dances. Eventually signals for music to cut out. To audience:

Hello.

They will likely respond.

He keeps moving.

If you don't mind I'm gonna move around.

Trying to calm himself.

I'm a little nervous— "If you don't mind." Why would you mind? You're here of your own volition. Or maybe you were dragged here, I don't know. *(Some more moving.)* Okay. *(Trying to calm.)* Okay.

Breathes. Asks for a moment. Breathes. Is ready. Is not ready. Asks for a moment. Disappointed in himself. Breathes. Etc. Until, finally:

I have cancer.

There.

My days are numbered and I'm spending them with you.

What else about me…

My father beat me, my mother beat me, my brother beat me. Good thing I came from such a small family.

That's a joke. Actually, my father was a charming and beloved man, though he did tyrannize me, my mother was a delightful fruitcake, though she did neglect me, and my brother is dear to my heart to this day, though he did beat me.

I have two daughters (have). At the elder daughter's Bat Mitzvah, the younger daughter gave a speech, and at some point in her speech—she was eight at the time—at one point she said, "If you're enjoying my speech, please give me a whoopa whoopa!" And the people gave her a whoopa whoopa!

So to honour my daughter and for the pleasure of the theatre gods, please give me a whoopa whoopa!

Audience obliges.

Bless your hearts.

Light on audience out.

He walks to sit in chair.

Slide: CT scan.

The lungs of the hero of our story, the hero being the fellow who goes by the same name as me, which is almost the same thing as me, but it isn't. Those are his lungs. These *(Big breath in.)* are mine.

However, we both have cancer, which has been deemed terminal. In August of 2018 we were diagnosed with stage four lung cancer. But it's not the kind you get from smoking, let it be known, we did not do this to ourself. I didn't. He may have with the shenanigans he got up to.

Light shift. Slide: "DAY 0—Arrival"

Sound of car on highway.

He walks to centre stage.

April 2019, eight months after diagnosis, and I'm driving to a ten-day Vipassana meditation retreat in Montebello, Quebec. It's bilingual. I'm not worried about my French, but I am worried about my health. Two weeks ago, I had a pericardial tap—

fluid was drained from the sac around my heart, the pericardium—and it still hurts. Am I well enough?

Will I have the strength to endure ten brutal days of sitting in silence? The food is vegetarian. Will they serve enough protein, enough fat?— fat is very important for the absorption of the targeted therapy pills that are keeping me alive. And if I get sick, how will I get out of there, who will take me to the hospital, and what hospital? What will happen to my car? How will I get my car home?

My side hurts. Why? Is that the pericardium filling again, pressing against my heart? Or is it the driving? Yes, yes, it's gotta be the driving, I've been driving for hours, it's the position, it puts stress on the wound. Just calm down. *(Calming.)* Just arrive, get to your room, and when the time comes, begin.

Sound of driving abruptly ends.

I've arrived, I'm checking in, and they've assigned me a roommate, which distresses me, because I'd asked for a private room—

I was expecting a private room.

> *Recorded: "I'm sorry, but you've been assigned this room."*

Yes, but in other Vipassana retreats I've been to, they honour age, the elders get a single room.

> *Recorded: "We don't do it like that here."*

I really need a private room. *(Almost weeping.)* I have stage four lung cancer, and I don't think I can stay if I have to share a room.

> *Recorded: "We'll see what we can do."*

I played the cancer card. I've played it before... Welcome to my show.

Light and sound shift, sound of door closing.

I step into my room for the first time, and there he is: my roommate, sitting on his neatly made bed, his shoes placed pedantically together.

His first words: "I'm never sure whether to talk before these things begin. I err on the side of not."

"Me too" were my first words.

"And I like to have a fan going at night. White noise, and it circulates the air. If it annoys you just (*Unplugging gesture.*)"

"Thank you. And for me, sorry, but I'll have to pee a lot at night."

"Me too. The privileges of age."

Later. My request was met, and he was removed from my room.

Later. All male participants gather in the male lobby of the meditation hall.

Our names will be called, and one by one we will be taken into the hall and given our place. And then, noble silence will begin.

For ten days we will not talk to anyone. We're not supposed to look anyone in the eye, we're not supposed to gesture, communicate in any way. The impending silence makes me aware, acutely aware, of a desperate urge to speak, this urge to speak, to gossip, to connect, to let others know who I am, that I'm a decent guy, this need to belong. I feel it as it's about to be taken away from me, I feel it, (*With feeling.*) feel, feel.

But there we are. We linger in the lobby. Some of us are chatting. About what? Who's done this before, who's married, my wife also meditates, I've been to India, I've got hemorrhoids, God knows we love our chatting.

And it's interesting to note who stands where. The handsome fellow seems to attract a crowd. He's attractive, he attracts. I stay on the outside of things. I don't feel very attractive myself.

Over the coming days, I will form opinions of these people. I can't help it, I can't help making judgements, compulsively. I will assign each of them a nickname.

There's the little man who will sit beside me in the meditation hall, with his easy, kind and always available smile. I will give him the name François, after St. Francis.

There's the aforementioned handsome fellow, who I will name Jason the Handsome. He'll sit at the front of the hall with his perfect posture and his pashmina shawl.

Oh, here comes Fast Walker, glasses askew, running late, going nowhere in a hurry, breaking all the rules along the way.

There's the Dancer. He's young, he's lithe. He likes to stretch. His stretches are so delicious I can taste them deep in my own tissue.

I didn't notice him at the time, but Red Crocs must have been there. At first I called him the Pig, but that was my nasty brain which was soon corrected by my Buddha brain. Red Crocs because of his red Crocs. He's been assigned the room right next to mine, and I will hear and smell him for days before I actually see the red Crocs.

There's Death Waits—he looks like a friend of mine. Pale, wears black, he will take his scythe and skedaddle after a few days. There's the hooded García Lorca, a moody show-off. There's the Bell Jar, a man in the shape of sadness. And the Regurgitator. His name emerged at lunch one day.

I stand there waiting. My hip really hurts, and never mind the hemorrhoids. They all chat with a quiet energy and a mighty expectation. Everyone seems so young. Nobody seems to want to stand beside me.

My ex-roommate stands alone. Already I fear his judgement.

If you were here you'd see Sexy Sari Guy, The Monk, Our Lady of the Flowers, but you're not here, you're at a play!

Light shift.

I did not do this to myself.

Myself. What is this self anyway? Anyway, anyway, that is far too much to get into at the moment. My future self may elaborate.

The first days after diagnosis were filled with dread, dread, a vast empty desert, with no language but one word: dread.

But I was dying in that desert, and so I had to turn my thoughts to what to do, how to proceed, how to do this dying thing—this living dying thing—how to do it right, whatever that means. For my daughters. My daughters would be watching me, they'd be living through it with me. I told them that I would fight. I wanted them to feel confident in my strength, that I was doing everything in my power to remain in their lives. Two weeks later my elder daughter sat me down and told me: "Sister and I have been talking, Dad, and we want you to know; if you're too tired, if it's too hard, you don't have to fight. Not for us."

Pause.

Sweet things like that emerge from the blessings of this disease. There are other things, like since the diagnosis, my daughters return my phone calls, which is nice. And also, here we all are, together again. Finally. Finally. Finally.

Audience light.

Let us say that space and time are infinite. If space and time are infinite, there are infinite possibilities, so it is almost a certainty that there exists an exact replica of our planet elsewhere, and every imaginable variation of our planet. Of me. Of you.

So let's say that one of those planets is exactly like this one. The only difference is that on that planet, at this very moment, a man like me, so much like me he may as well be me, closes his eyes—

Does so.

Does a little dance—

Does so.

And when he opens his eyes he no longer has cancer.

Opens eyes. Pause. Disappointment.

He closes his eyes—

Does so. Does a little dance.

And before he can open his eyes—

Sudden bus horn, big lights, big crash—

Lights restore.

I have terminal cancer, though a bus may get me first. So it's not necessarily terminal, it's more incurable. But of the many things on earth trying to kill me, cancer will probably win.

I'm sure you have a lot of questions, like precisely what kind of incurable lung cancer do you have? Are you scared? What's in your back pocket?

Reaches for something in back pocket. Shows:

A tooth.

Then a piece of paper. Reads:

Veggie stock. Jalapeno. Cilantro. Oatmeal…

Another piece of paper. He reads, not aloud, then teasingly puts it in his back pocket.

Audience light out.

Why did you go on a meditation retreat? (Thanks for asking) I want to die well. I want to fix myself.

I want to sit for ten days in silence, listen to the voices and quiet them. I want to be free of anger and hatred, of ego, of fear. I want to die free of fear. Free. Oh, freedom. Great feckless freedom: embedded in constitutions, shouted in street riots and intoned with soaring spirit in song, *(Sings.)* Freedom, oh, Freedom!

And I've learned freedom is nothing without discipline. But the mind is a monkey, and I am here to tame it, so that when I am lying on my deathbed I will be at peace and full of love.

Does that mean anything? I don't know. I have faith that it does. Somehow. That's my wild faith.

And by the way, cancer is okay. I don't want you to get the idea that it's all doom and gloom, lots of good things happen here on planet cancer. For instance, since the diagnosis my daughters return my phone calls—now I know I said that before but I like saying it so much I said it twice. I can't always answer because of side effects like fatigue or constipation or fear of dying, but they call.

When I eat out people often pick up the check, which is nice. And people are very generous: "If there's anything you need, anything I can do, just let me know, anytime, I'll be there, anytime—third week in June is best, I'm a bit busy till then." I understand, people are busy, at least they offer. I get lots of big hugs with "How *are* you?" which is a little annoying. At least "How *are* you?" clarifies they know I have cancer. Some people offer a neutral "How are you?" and I have no idea if the person knows I have cancer. So I disarm them by saying: "I'm dying," and then they disarm me by saying "Aren't we all?" No, actually, no, some of us are dying MORE than others. That is one thing not to say to someone with a terminal illness: "We're all dying." No, no, I'm fucking dying, I've got shitty fucking terminal cancer, at least let me feel special. "We're all dying." Fuck off. *(Immediate apology.)* Sorry.

Anyway, lots of perks, lots of perks, the best is, and I mean this, lots of love coming my way. The kind of love that… I don't get any sex out of it.

Dating prospects have plummeted. You wanna hear my dating profile? Single white male, 63, over-educated, under-employed artist with health issues, seeks special pal. Has car, likes to go to bed early, not interested in a long-term relationship.

And—oh—if you're talking to a citizen of Incurable Cancer Land about books, let me give you a piece of advice: Do not recommend a book casually. If you're going to suggest a book, it better be a fucking good book.

Finally, please don't ask me "Is there anything special you want to do before you die, anything on your bucket list?" I hate that bucket list bullshit, it makes me nauseous. Give me the bucket so I can puke in it. Oh, actually, there is something I'd like to do before I die: Puke in that goddam bucket list bucket.

A few tips for y'all.

Light shift.

Back in the lobby. We mill about waiting for our names to be called, our beautiful names. I saunter over to the group, trying to look important in my deportment, and stand by the side of my ex-roommate, and I believe he guffawed, or harrumphed. As if to say "Too late to make nice with me, Monsieur."

A name was called. Tony Small. He moved. That was his name. Mine was called soon after. No mistaking my name, that's me. The name written on the labels of my T-shirts at summer camp, on my report cards at Upper Canada College, on my driver's licence, the name to be exalted at my memorial service—if there is one—the name written in marker on my food container, my special plastic food container in the dining room as I have special dietary needs, as I have special needs, Tony Small. I'm dying of cancer, there was a reason I asked for a solo room, I have needs: I have my pills and the green tea in the morning and the little brazil nuts and various other foods I'm not supposed to eat in my room, and there's the constipation and the urothelial carcinoma—that's a second cancer I have, which blocks my ureter so I have to pee at night a lot, a *lot*, beyond the privileges of age. I have these special needs, it was nothing personal, Tony Small. I'm not your enemy. I'm not your enemy!

(Plaintively.) Now I have an enemy.

Pause. He walks toward chair, upstage right, and moves it centre stage as he speaks.

On the retreat you're not supposed to write. You're not supposed to bring a writing implement, but I did and I will write. But I will only allow myself to write about three things:

meditation, cancer, and Other People.

He sits. Sound of a bell.

The noble silence begins.

Light shift.

In the meditation hall, there is a men's side and a women's side. I'm on the men's side. There is a teacher on each side, facing the meditators. On our side, there are five rows with men sitting on the floor, and two rows in chairs *(Indicates to left.)* for those who prefer not to sit on the floor, which I prefer because sitting cross-legged on the floor for twelve hours a day causes great pain, consternation and an overwhelming sense of failure.

There he is, in a chair, a row ahead and to the left, my enemy. Tony Small. I study my enemy—that's an exaggeration. I'm aware of him. His funny little toque, his little sweaty face. He looks nervous, my enemy. I feel competitive. Maybe I'll learn something from him—

We hear Goinka.

And the meditation begins.

It's the voice of our deceased guru Goinka, dead now for eight years.

So you listen to his dead voice through the speakers and he leads us through a vow, which we all say together—I don't, I'm not much of a joiner—and then he gives us our meditation instructions, he talks us through our first meditation. You see, it's very structured. Our day is very structured, from 4:00 in the morning when the bell rings till 9:30 at night when it's lights out. The only thing they can't structure, nor do they want to, is your thought.

So we meditate. I sit there and breathe, all we do is breathe. We're asked to focus our attention on our breath. But armies of thoughts invade my mind, the wild monkey screams through the forest, and eventually, after dinner—my dinner from the aforementioned plastic container—after some pills, and a walk and perusal of the other meditators—there's The Dancer doing his marvellous stretches, there's Death Waits looking down at his Birkenstocks, there's Jason the Handsome looking handsome, there's the Bell Jar doing nothing—after the walk, and one more meditation, the day ends.

In the night I wake up, and I don't feel well. It's hot, I'm hot, it's very hot, my brain's on fire and my chest doesn't feel right, something's wrong. I sit on the end of my bed, and my head is dizzy, I'm sweating. I'm sick again. How am I going to get to a hospital, how am I gonna get my car home, I knew I shouldn't have come, what do I do, my head is spinning, can I even get up? I get up. I'm dizzy, I'm so hot, I'm dying. I go to the window and open it, I'm burning up, the room begins to cool, and I begin to cool down, I cool down…and I'm okay. I'm fine, I'm fine. The room was hot, but now it's not, and I'm fine. Never mind. False alarm. *Pardonnez-moi.*

So from then on I decide to stop worrying. Don't worry.

Lies down.

Our hero lays in bed. He thinks about how there is no God to remember any of this, that he will disappear without a trace. He worries about tomorrow's food and thinks about Her, who he loved, or loves, "But is love the right word?" He remembers dancing in the streets with her in that town in India, and he recedes, and recedes, and eventually… *(Falls asleep.)*

Rises, sits cross-legged on the floor. A moment with the audience.

Imre Kertész wrote a novel, *Fatelessness*. It's a semi-autobiographical tale about a fifteen-year-old Hungarian boy and his experience in the Holocaust. The boy is Jewish, but he resents being Jewish, because he doesn't really lead a Jewish life and yet he has to suffer the indignities of being Jewish in Budapest in 1943. His father is about to be hauled off to a work camp, and the boy gives him a hug and cries, and realizes that he doesn't cry because he feels any grief, he cries because he thinks he's supposed to. And when he himself is told he's going to the work camps, he's excited. He thinks the yellow star is cool. He likes Germans, he likes the way they dress, he likes their black boots, and he's excited to travel with his pals. Eventually he ends up in the concentration camp at Buchenwald.

What I find so remarkable about Kertész's novel is that the boy never has any idea about "the Holocaust." The word had yet to be invented. He has zero historical perspective, he was just in it, as we are in this, living each day, one step at a time, and some days, amidst the horror and death, there was even pleasure. He ends up with typhoid and he's lying in bed in the squalid infirmary, and outside his window someone has planted tulips. As he weakens, he fears for his life, and looking out the window at the tulips he says a kind of prayer: "Dear God, let me live just one more day in this beautiful concentration camp."

Just one more day.

My grandfather was born in the 1880s into a Jewish family, in Turek, Poland.

They specialized in making wedding dresses in Turek. His whole family—my family—was murdered in the Holocaust. My father was in the

American army that liberated Buchenwald. I've seen the photos, lots of photos. All those bodies piled high, each body formerly a person, with a name. Each with the miracle of their own singular experience, and now nameless.

My family. My name. My body— "My body," what a strange phrase, "my body," *(Forcefully touching his body.)* as if I own it, *my* body. *My* body on *my* stage in *my* theatre in *my* town, all in my little *yiddisher kopf*. And this is how I will die my death; I will be lying on my death bed, with a smile on my face—

Sudden bus horn, big lights, big crash—

Lights restore.

Pause. Light shift.

The morning bell and slide: "DAY 1"

Day 1. Wake up, have my green tea, do some tai chi, 4:30 a.m., meditate.

First is anapana, the meditation on the breath, just concentrate on the breath.

Incoming breath, outgoing breath. But the mind thinks, so you're instructed to—if the mind thinks—that's okay, just go back to the breath. Don't judge, don't be disappointed, just "smilingly" go back to the breath.

But I think. And I begin to notice what I'm thinking about, like Robert Lepage's last show which I really liked, so I begin to make myself "don't" promises, things to "don't" think about, like don't think about Lepage, and don't think about Her. But I think about Her, so I slam the door on Her, and I think about Lepage, so I slam the door on Lepage. But I think "That's a little violent," so I pick them both up very gently and place them in lawn chairs in a lovely little garden wet with rain, and Robert lounges and spins a lotus flower on his fingertip, and she has a martini, which could be trouble later, and I'm afraid now that I've placed them there together, they'll have sex. I think everyone wants to have sex with her now that she doesn't want to have sex with me, but Robert is gay, and it doesn't matter anyway because he's lounging in a chair spinning a lotus flower on his fingertip IN MY HEAD.

So this idyll of a garden scene, I will it away. Discipline. Back to the breath—but where did the garden go?—back to the breath—but the garden is so—back to the breath! Smilingly.

6:00 a.m., breakfast, which is delicious, then incoming breath, outgoing breath, then a walk, then incoming breath, outgoing breath.

Then lunch!

I have my food. Others are lined up for the buffet. Some are already sitting at tables. Who do I sit beside? There's Tony Small. No, thank you.

I want the table by the window that looks out at the trees. I want so much.

And mindlessly I sit beside Jason the Handsome.

Then back to the hall for more incoming breath, outgoing breath,

and then dinner! Which is no more than an orange for civilians, but because of my special status, I eat from the plastic container with my name on it, in the special needs room. There's the Regurgitator, bent over his food. I don't sit beside him, he isn't attractive. He makes funny noises when he eats, he regurgitates his food.

Then I nip to my room for a nap, then back to the hall for more meditation, then the evening discourse from Goinka. Impatience creeps into my bones. And then one more f'n fucking meditation.

And the day ends, as a day will do. It's lights out at 9:30—our hero extinguishes his lamp at 9:17. He tucks between the cool sheets and his eyes close and there are thoughts and thoughts and slowly he becomes that other self, the one that sleeps. And maybe the other one, the one that dreams.

Lights on audience.

Primo Levi tells this story:

Stands and approaches audience.

He was in Auschwitz, it was winter, he was in his cell and he was thirsty. He spies an icicle hanging outside his window. He reaches out and breaks it off, and as he brings it to his mouth to slake his thirst, a passing guard whacks it out of his hand.

He's shocked. He gathers himself, and asks the guard, "Why?" "Why? *Warum? Hier ist kein warum.* There is no why here."

Why. Why indeed. Why me? Why do I have terminal cancer? I see other members of my tribe, the cancer tribe, at the Cancer Hospital, in waiting rooms, waiting to be infused, poked, scanned, slashed. And some of them are younger than me. A lot younger than me.

And some are my age, but maybe they've not had the life I've had, which was not bad, so why not me? I've lived a life. I've paddled great northern rivers, I've done acid in Paris, man, I've won a Dora, and I've had love, great love. So why not me? Why that young person? Why anyone? Why cancer? Why death? Why?

There is no "why" here.

Lights fade on audience.

Sits.

A bell, with slide: "DAY 2"

Here in Montebello, the instructions are given in English and then French. First Goinka, and then his translator. I like listening to the French. My French is pretty good. As I listen, I think, it's good to think in another language, you think differently in a different language, and then I realize "That's not your thought, you got that from a book." I continue to listen to the translation and then I wonder "How are the French meditators getting on?" and then I find fault with the translation, and then remember: back to the breath. Don't judge. Back to the breath.

Breathe.

But then I have a conversation with Her—well, it's not really a conversation, I do all the talking.

But I think about Her and the jewel box and—don't think about Her. Breathe.

But then I have lurid sexual fantasies—don't think about sex. Breathe.

Then I think about Abraham, Isaac and Jacob. I wonder when Abraham takes Isaac up the mountain—don't think about the patriarchs. Breathe.

We breathe, François, Jason the Handsome, Tony Small, all of us, we're instructed to narrow our focus to the area below the nostril and above the upper lip and pay attention to the sensation of the breathing there. At first I feel it, the little patch of flesh feels cool when I breathe in, and warm when I breathe out. It's very subtle, the concentration is good. But the hours pass, the mind slips, and the nose slides. My eyes are closed, all I see is nose. It elongates, then it crawls up my face onto my forehead, then it hovers above me in dark space. It expands as big as the meditation hall, it contracts, a hummingbird, it darts over to the women's side and darts back, it expands and inhales whole star systems, then drips, drips in a dense fog. It calcifies, and then it plummets into a deep dark void, my chair is empty, the nose under me now, in a swamp, a scuttling bug, a battle ship, a mandala, a tetrahedron… such shapes, such visions. A mind out of control.

That's my mind. My mind. My mind. Mind…

Sound loop of "mind," he repeats "mind" on top of loop. Sudden end.

I walk after meditation. There's Tony Small. I try to be nice in his presence, I try to project an air of conviviality and caring for my fellow human, to counter whatever foul opinion he has constructed of me. I constantly rehearse my explanation to him as to why I had him removed from my room: "Listen, I have health issues"—health issues, c'mon, be bold—"Listen, I have stage four lung cancer, Tony, and I do things, I cheat, and it would have been distracting for you, and this may be my last Vipassana retreat before I die, Tony. Tony. Tony Small."

We breathe. Day one, day two, day three, we breathe, concentrating on that little field of dreams below the nostrils. Breath in… breath out… breath in… breath out. The breath so light, the sensation so subtle, the concentration consistent…

Ah.

Success.

I knew immediately that hubris would slap my face.

Ya see, when you have a successful meditation you want to repeat it, but it cannot be repeated. The breath of now is now, you can't take it forward. You want the feeling of past success, you want it, but you don't get it, because it's not repeatable. And so your will is thwarted, and you get frustrated, and angry, and really angry and angry, *(Falls to his knees in increasing rage.)* it ruins your day, and hours and hours and days can pass before concentration finally graces you again with its ease and presence.

Has calmed. Moment.

Stands, then sits in chair.

Sound of bell and slide: "DAY 4"

We move on to Vipassana meditation. For Vipassana, we are instructed by the dead voice of Goinka to move our attention to the top of our heads, and to be aware of any sensation we're feeling there—feeling, sensation, what's the difference? They're just words; feeling, sensation, feeling, *feeling,* anyway—we the meditators are told to scan our bodies for sensation, from the top of the head to the tips of the toes. As you scan you may feel what Goinka calls unpleasant solidified gross sensations, i.e., pain, on some parts of the body, or all over the body. You may experience no sensations, or you may experience a pleasant sensation, a kind of "tingling" on some parts of the body, or a free flow of "tingling" all over the body.

Vipassana meditation, scan the body. That's it.

And so I sit in my chair and meditate.

Music.

For hours. For days. And as the mind swings from tree to tree, I scan my body: My scalp, my forehead, the pain in my shoulder, I'm stepping on a plane on my way to see Her—a different Her, this is years ago—and as I step on the plane she's drinking with another guy, and later, as I fly towards her, they're fucking, in our hotel room, and I'm just an hour away. Why? I loved her. Why? And I feel this ancient jealousy, and I remember, just observe it, just observe—but then a rage emerges, and it's the rage of a seven-year-old boy. The tantrums I had when I was seven: Throwing chairs, punching windows, tearing down curtains. I was the youngest, I was the weakest, I was the lowest, I always lost. There was no one to take my side, no one to defend me, no one saw my needs. What about me, I'm seven. *(Pleading.)* Someone help me, someone see me. See me!

Pause. Lights on audience.

More cancer etiquette?... Okay.

He stands and moves towards audience.

When talking to we cancer people, please don't suggest the miracle cure of grape seed extract that your daughter's Pilates teacher's dog walker knows about. Or talk to me about that rock star who was cured of pancreatic cancer by eating changa mushrooms, and don't suggest six weeks at the Gerson Institute, because I've heard it all and I don't have time to chase down every grape seed cure, and I don't have pancreatic cancer, I have a different malady with a very special mutation of which you've probably never heard and of which I have become something of a lay expert, and as far as changa mushrooms go I'm already taking reishi mushrooms which is one of the reasons I need my private room, Tony Small!

Tony Small has an umbrella he uses when it rains. He puts it in his spot in the foyer before he enters the chamber. Right there. Balanced. His umbrella. It keeps him dry.

The umbrella is him, it's an assertion of self. Tony and his umbrella.

He sits.

The picture begins to form of a man with eccentric habits. He seems very fussy, very alone in the world, maybe too alone to form great bonds of love and intimacy, his habits a kind of cloak to the messy spontaneity of interaction. Which is where we lose our personalities, in orgies of interaction. Perhaps his loneliness is the only way he can preserve his personality.

Will I apologize to him when this is over? Will it help him in any way? Will it help me?

I look at him often. I look at him, urging him to forgive me. But he is so uncomfortable in his meditation—but never mind, close your eyes, don't think of Lepage, and scan the body—at dinner I see Tony's face. It seems smaller. Sad. Lost.

Tony Small.

Lou Reed's "Sad Song" emerges. He begins to sing along. With increasing verve. Then the sound cuts out.

My father, in his last days, was unable to speak. But not speaking and not hearing are not the same thing. In his death chamber, loved ones spoke as if he couldn't hear, as if he were already gone, as if it didn't matter what was said. Maybe he could hear, maybe not, I don't know.

But for me, I want to make it very clear: If I have reached the point where I can no longer speak, please, conduct yourselves as if I can hear everything. Take the chance that I can. That's what I would like. And I recommend you ask for the same…

Though some of you may die suddenly: Some by fire, some by fentanyl, some by a lover's hand, some by some command. Some of you may get hit by that bus that's been wandering around this theatre. But many of you *will* die the slowish way, falling silent for a couple of days, less breath, less breath, vomit, then death. I hope you are surrounded by love, the silence only broken with caring words, whether grief-stricken or lighthearted, the silence full of attention to your great event: Your sacred final breath.

Scan the body.

He scans for an instant.

Or the room is full of laughter and mirth and circus clowns and they forget about you and everyone has already moved on, that's fine too, whatever, it doesn't really matter, I don't know, I don't know, I'm no expert just because I'm dying of cancer, I don't mean to tell you what to think or say. I certainly don't want to tell you how to die. If you die screaming in agony and utterly alone, who's to say that's a bad death? There are no bad deaths, they're all good deaths.

Still today. Scan the body.

Scans for an instant.

"Sad song, sad song," Lou Reed is so—scan the body.

Scans.

My thigh, my calf, my foot's asleep—"Sad song, sad song," why is that song so sad? Three chords, D E G, so sad, so simple—well, it's not so simple. The three chords have a history, there's the history of harmony. There's Lou Reed's guitar, the minds that created the very idea of a guitar, the hands that fashioned the soundboard, the neck, the frets, the um, I don't know what anything else is called on a guitar, there's the tree and the soil it grew in, the chestnut or whatever a Gibson is made of, there's Lou Reed's bony fingers, the floor he crawled on as a babe, his mother's voice, all the mothers—scan the body.

Scans for an instant.

Of note (I'll scan later): The Tibetan Buddhists believe that in the eons of lives we have already lived, every human on earth has, in one of our past lives, been our mother. They've loved and nurtured us as a mother, and so we owe everyone gratitude.

Imagine. Each of you has been my mother. In one life, Adolph Eichmann was my mother, so please don't hate me, Tony Small, I have stage four lung cancer and I need my own room, and you don't know what it's like to have Adolph Eichmann as a mother. Please, it wasn't personal. I don't know you, I don't know you at all, Tony Small, and in one life in this infinite realm of the infinite I was *your* mother and I loved you so. I love you now. And I hate you. No love without hate. Oh, that's so banal. But true. *(He screams.)* Scan the body.

Scans for a moment.

(Flatulence.) Sorry. What is that? Maybe it's the flax they serve at meditation buffet. Tomorrow I won't eat—don't think about food.

That's a lot of "don'ts" to track: Don't think about food, don't think about Lepage—don't think about don't.

Tries to scan for a moment.

I can hear François as I meditate, his stomach. My neighbour man, *mon voisin, mon semblable, mon frère*. I can hear each burp, slurp, snort, swallow, lick. I can hear him hearing me: My flatulence and my attempts to hide my flatulence, my every sigh and disappointment, every shift, every sound. Such an intimate sharing of struggle, so intimate. My lover François. My sweet François.

Not to mention the hemorrhoids, which is a problem when you sit for 69 hours a day. Everything hurts. We're instructed to observe the hurt objectively, don't identify with the hurt, just observe. And sometimes it melts away. For a moment. Then more hurt, then more meditation, then more hurt, then lunch! There's the Bell Jar, a mountain of flesh on a bench, his plate piled high. There's Jason the Handsome—I'm developing a little theory about him. I think he's polyamorous. That pashmina shawl of his was a gift from his Slovakian lover he met in Kashmir, on a Harley Davidson—then more meditation, more hurt, the discourse, more hurt, and finally bedtime.

I lay down and scan my body, and think about the prohibition against killing. Before we begin the retreat we take an ethical vow, to abstain from the following five things:

Killing, stealing, lying, the taking of intoxicants and… *(Rude gesture as he tries to remember, then dismisses.)* the fifth one. The prohibition against killing. That means vegetarian food and *(Kills a mosquito.)* none of that. But I have killed, and I will kill again. What have I killed?

Mosquitoes, flies, cockroaches, I once killed a hamster to put it out of its misery, once ran over a cat late at night on a road in County Cork—I was driving too fast—indirectly killed countless cows, chickens, fish, took antibiotics to kill gonococcus, killed the enthusiasm of friends, slaughtered a marriage, infected my children with the fatal disease of life, and murdered piles of time.

This cancer body…

And that day's self lays in bed and thinks, and fantasizes that he collects a single tear from all eight billion of us who are here, in a jar. He has a little cry and adds his own tear. He takes that jar of tears to a mountaintop in the Yukon, he lays down and waits for summer solstice to arrive. And when it does, as the sun sets, he shakes the tears, takes a sip, swallows. And he feels the most exquisite…

emptiness.

And then he wanders off into the land of unremembered dreams.

Bell and slide: "DAY 5"

Day… whatever. As I scan my body these memories. I'm not sure what they mean, memories of my father or indiscretions or memories of innocent moments—if there is such a thing as the memory of an innocent moment, since the moment, once lived, loses its innocence—oh, scan the body.

He scans for a moment.

And then Goinka talks us through all the possible sensations we might experience as we scan: Hot. Cold. Heavy. Light. Wet. Dry. Scratching. Throbbing. Tingling. Hot. Cold—over and over. And then, he takes us through the body, part by part, moving down, from the top of the head to the tips of the toes: The scalp, the forehead, the eyes, the cheeks—yes, I know you're moving down one part at a time, that's very clear to me now—the neck, the chest, the back—does the back have parts, how do I carve the back up? And for some reason he's mum on the penis and the vagina. Aren't they part of one part at a time? All of a sudden Goinka's gone prude—yes the thigh, yes the calf is next, yes I know, shut up, shut up. Let me do it my way. Let me do it my way or I won't feel a single sensation: No hot no cold no wet no dry no ache no throb no tangle no tingle no nothing. Leave me be, shut up, and LET ME DO IT MY WAY!

And then I go back to my room to write all that down, secretly, with my forbidden implement. So not only am I a cheatin' liar, but my attention is now fixated on writing, on achieving something, and also now I'm Mr. Sneaky Cheeks: How to hide the sound of the zipper that tells Red Crocs next door that I'm opening my suitcase to get my notepad, or how to hide the sound of the page turning, or how to hide the sound of my ego pouring out of my pen. And later, I actually interrupt a meditation and run back to my room to record my profoundly inconsequential thoughts. And so I vow to stop writing. Don't write.

Gesture of breaking pen and throwing it on floor. Pause.

Looks at pen, then away. Waits. Looks at pen. Waits. Picks up pen. Writes.

Con-sti-pa-tion. Constipation. I was constipated.

Sound of bell and slide: "DAY 6"

After six days I finally had a shit. It was so hard, I literally had to dig it out with my fingers. I'm sitting on the toilet (what else) I'm trying not to make too much noise because these walls are cheap, but it's like giving birth, and when the thing finally comes out it is as compact as a piece of coal that could heat a house for days. Then I picture the family gathered 'round the hearth, warming our hands by the heat of my waste, and I'm the dad telling once-upon-a-time princess dragon kind of stories. A couple of days later the little one—she's so sweet—she says to me "Daddy, it's cold in here, can we put another one of your cweations on the fire?" "I'm working on it, Daddy won't be shitting for another couple of days." "Oh Daddy. We're wooting fo' you, we're wooting fo' you." At least I got the whole family wootin' for me—scan the body.

He scans.

My right buttock, my left buttock, her left buttock—don't think about Her. My right thigh, my mother's thighs. My mother. Her hand, her wrist, her veins were like mine, she had a charm bracelet, with a tiny trombone I pretended to blow and puffed out my cheeks like Louis Armstrong and that would make her laugh. My mother. My father. There were no civil conversations between my parents, neither before the divorce nor after. My father's ashes are still in my kitchen cupboard. I should sprinkle them on my mother's grave, so they can be together again, consigned to oblivion together, so they can bicker forever in the raging fires of hell.

I'm not really angry at my parents anymore—I realize—what I feel is sorrow for that little boy who had the same name as me, who raged against the curtains.

Light shift.

Stands and moves to audience.

Takes the paper out of his back pocket. Looks at it.

When you first enter the meditation chamber, your ten-day prison, there is a name tag waiting for you at your cushion or chair. For some reason I kept mine. For some reason, here it is.

I'm trying not to be my "self" but there's my name screaming at me every time I sit.

"DANIEL BROOKS"

But the self that name represents is apparently an illusion, and the self who just said that is just another self. Beyond every self is another self. Outside of every circle you can draw another circle. Beneath every deep is a deeper deep.

I am many selves. I am a night self, and my night self likes to clean and prepare the kitchen for my morning self, so that in the morning, my morning self is always grateful. I hope that if my various selves treat each other well, they will develop the habit of treating others with equal kindness.

He looks at the paper.

We are all many selves. I'm a father self. I have two daughters, and I will die without knowing what becomes of them. I will not know their destiny. So I've asked them, on the anniversary of my death, to observe a ritual. On each anniversary, I've asked them to tell me what's happened to them in the past year, "What's goin' on, my darlings?" so they can hear the heartbeat of their own lives. And also, as a way of keeping me alive.

Light shift as he sits.

Still Day 6. My various selves continue to meditate for hour after hour.

Back in my room, I can hear Red Crocs through the cheap wall:

"O la la la la la la." Some bags are shuffled. What's he doing in there? Is he packing his bags to leave? People leave. Death Waits, who seemed so unhappy, suddenly I realize he's gone. But Red Crocs, what's he feeling? I can hear he's suffering. I seem not to care. My concern? Does he hear the ball rolling in my ballpoint pen? Does he wonder about me? He can't imagine that I'm writing for an audience, that I will speak the words I am writing, how could he? But what is he thinking about right now? Taxes? Death? Hemorrhoids?

Goinka chanting loud.

Goinka introduces the word "equanimity."

There is pleasure and there is pain. Both—

He stands to move closer to audience, fighting the volume of the chanting.

Both pleasure and pain have the same nature, the nature of arising, then passing away. Pleasure arises, but sooner or later passes away. Pain arises, but sooner or later it passes away. Both are impermanent. So why have craving for pleasure, why have an aversion to pain, when neither lasts? And so we are encouraged to observe both pleasure and pain with equanimity.

Equanimity, equan—

Goinka still chanting.

Those fucking speakers are too fucking loud, the chanting is too loud!

I ask the teacher to lower the volume: "The volume is just another obstacle to be overcome with equanimity." Okay, fine, equanimity all the way.

Later, when I'm on a break and no one's looking, I pivot the speaker up.

Volume of chanting reduces significantly.

Problem solved, another obstacle overcome with equanimity.

(As he sits.) I head out on my walk and there's The Bell Jar, his depression spreads out on a bench, and in my nastiness I think he's dreaming of cake. But he's so young, his laziness is impressive—but so is my lack of equanimity. I step out of the woods. The Dancer's watching me. I have an urge to perform for him, to impress him. I do some tai chi.

Does tai chi in chair.

Watch me… watch me…this hunger for attention, this endless performance. Don't perform. Stop performing! How?

His body continues to perform. A physical struggle, then:

Scan the body, scan the body.

Scans for an instant.

Don't think about Her—I will think about Her—don't think about Her—I will think about Her, and I will think about the jewel box.

The jewel box, morning caresses before words intervene, then waves of agreement and breath, breath and breath, and holy union. And that hotel room in Mumbai, she rolling onto him, he into her, and knowing her again by the endless light of the midnight sun, may all be blessed with such a night, with such a body, her body to which he bows in solemn defeat, gladly surrendering to its glorious victory, swallowed by its all in all, its flavours and textures and undulating organs, its sweet sweet offerings, such a tactic of total victory, he surrenders, he surrenders, on the mound and in the wet and holy tomb of desire where all his selves will die in her arms my love, my love, my love…

Pause.

"The Death of Ivan Ilyich." Tolstoy's story. Ivan is dying. His wife is impatient for his death. His daughter "The sooner the better." His friends at the club wonder who will get his job, and his "best friend" the day of his death is more concerned with that evening's card game than mourning the death of his friend or paying respects to his widow, and everyone thinks only of themselves. Okay, sure, we're all selfish, but it's really a matter of emphasis.

Tolstoy emphasizes the corrupted soul. But surely he could have emphasized the love the wife had for her husband, surely there was love. And we have the freedom to emphasize what we want: How I wanted to grow old with Her, and watch her body watch my body watch her body genuinely age, together, how we would see beauty in fading flesh. But I'm not going to grow old. *(Hits his body.)* It can't.

But Tolstoy's story is not about how Ivan died, it's about how he lived. It's the story about a man who has lived to please other people, and it has corrupted his Christian soul. Perhaps that's what I'm doing, trying to please you with my "performing." But it's a matter of emphasis. I could also emphasize the love in my heart, and how the love for others redeems me. And it does. Thank you for being here. You are doing me a great service.

Light shift.

Still Day 6. Ole Red Crocs is carrying tea into his bedroom, that's a no-no, "You're bad." 4:00 p.m., he's snoring, he's snoring and I'm trying to meditate. Pig! I think that often: "Pig, idiot, moron," when someone is smacking their lips, like The Regurgitator, or coughing open-mouthed, like García Lorca. What is the origin of this aversion: "Idiot, jerk, asshole." He may have a reason that he smacks his lips. Maybe he's sick, maybe he has cancer. We're all the same, we are one people, one coughing, lip-smacking, loud-chewing, grunting, belching, stinking herd of annoyance. A gaggle of geese. A murder of crows. An annoyance of humans.

Scans a moment.

Why am I the only one not getting tingling sensations? I want to tingle. I want to tingle before I die—equanimity.

Scans a moment.

I tell my Best Friend—why him, why is he the one at my bedside as my time comes to a halt? It's just that way—I ask him, "When the time comes, will you hold my hand, quietly, without ceremony, with a gentle, divine pressure, will you do that for me?"

I always picture the prolonged, gentle vigil: Family and friends by my bedside, a line-up of admirers out the door, down the hall of the hospital ward, down the stairs and out into the street, the doctors and nurses very impressed, "He must be loved."

But things may go downhill quickly.

I may cease alone, and there may be pain and struggle, screams and lamentations, all alone, without my people, without my daughters, and that will be as it is, I may cease alone.

I see that. I think I'm ready, ready for surprises. But can anyone really be ready, can anyone really know how they will be in the end? We can only prepare. And this is my preparation.

Bell and slide: "DAY 7"

I'm craving the tingle, and that overwhelms Day 7. Tingle, tingle: I feel the tingle, but it doesn't last, not for me. For me it gets interrupted by the ache in my shoulder or the pain in my hemorrhoids or François's gurgling stomach, or craving the tingle. Yesterday I felt the tingle, but today I feel nothing except a craving for yesterday's tingle. This poison of craving. Go away craving. Fuck off craving! Great, now I have an aversion to craving.

Music.

I go for a walk. There's Fast Walker, he's walking fast. He said thank you to me when I opened a door for him. Thank you? You're not supposed to say anything. And he spends a lot of time leering at the women's side of the hall. Fast Walker irritates me to my testes. Yes! I am the prosecution in a court of law that enforces nothing and is recognized by no one, in a state whose only natural resources are craving and aversion, and Fast Walker averts me!

Bell and slide: "DAY 8"

It's morning. I emerge from the death of sleep without a clue as to why I should be alive today, feeling a kind of withering ache—observe it with equanimity, equanimity—all I want is a little tingle, for God's sake, a little ting—equanimity, equanim—and I can out-meditate every last one of them. 4:30 a.m. every morning, I'm there in the meditation hall, one of only a handful of warriors. And when Jason the Handsome, meditating up front, leaves, I stay. He exits down the row and sees me outlast him. Another victory. Useless victories pile up all life long.

I shit, it's the first in two days. It required a C-section. It was like shitting a toddler, like shitting Arnold Schwarzenegger.

Day 8 ain't going so well.

And my mind? Mere mind. Mere mind, mere mind mind...

Another sound loop. He harmonizes with himself. Then sound cuts suddenly.

Breakfast. There's García Lorca stretched out on a bench—that's okay, I don't care. I don't care who I sit beside anymore. There's Tony Small, in my favourite spot by the window, staring out.

I sit, content that no one will join me. No one does.

I seem to be having trouble with equanimity.

I want this all to mean something. And at the same time, I want it to be over.

I have not learned a thing.

I meditate, but my concentration is failing. Between sits I watch the boys outside the meditation hall, they sit in the sun and wait in perfect geometric patterns.

Cancer changes your relationship with people. For instance, I know that when they see me they have no idea I am besieged by this thought:

"I have terminal cancer."

It separates me (I realize). It separates me.

Lunch. I sit beside Jason the Handsome. He keeps his food portions separate from one another. I should be concentrating on my breath, or the bare fact of chewing, or impermanence, but my attention is fixed on the neat arrangement of lentils and rice on his plate, the date square set aside, impatiently waiting to please his palate.

The final days are passing, comfortless, uneventful, except…

Bell and slide: "DAY 9"

Suddenly I begin to feel it. I feel the tingle. The tingle pours over my scalp and down my face, I feel the rapidity with which the tiniest particles of matter flicker in and out of existence. My stiff jaw tingles and melts away, the tingle pours down my neck, across my back, over my chest and into my lungs, into my heart, my vital organs. I tingle everywhere.

And outside of me, all those bodies: my best friends, my worst enemies, Tony Small, he feels pleasure and pain, arising and passing away, arising and eventually all will pass away, all the bodies: the faces, the greedy hands and empty stomachs, the shaking fists and broken hearts, Her beautiful eyes, all craving, all aversion, all ego, all personality, all joy, all will pass away. All forms: tiny trombones and hummingbirds and living rooms, all structures, all cities, all planets, all galaxies, all Gods, all up, all down, all before, all after, and all that is to come, all will pass away, leaving only the trace of a tingle…

(Very pleased.) I want to tell Her what I now know and—

(Not pleased.)—immediately that desire knocks me off the path.

I know nothing. And I'm still suffering. We all suffer; experience moulds everyone and we all suffer in our own way. So why should I have anger?

Well, the Regurgitator does swallow his own vomit, Red Crocs snores when I'm trying to sleep, someone left their shoes right in the middle of the hall where people are walking. I would never do that, it's not fair, why aren't these people behaving like me, what about me, I'm here, what about me? What about me? Me!

I want it, I want peace, I want the tingle, I want the sensation of simple being, I want it, I want enlightenment, I want it. Where did it go, where the fuck did it go? Give it back to me, please, please *(Weeping.)* Mummy, Mummy, please, *(Desperate and weeping.)* it's the last day of the retreat, please *(Irredeemable sobbing. Big breath.)*

Equanimity. *(Big breath.)*

Equanimity. *(Breath.)*

It's just a body. Meditating with the other bodies.

Sound of single goose.

And then high overhead, a goose flies by. It honks, we all hear it, and I wonder: Does that goose know that eighty silly meditators are listening to its conversation with the universe?

It's spring, glorious spring. The birds sing with desire. Without desire we wouldn't be here.

Springtime once again. Maybe our hero's last.

Stands. Walks upstage. Turns to audience.

I went to see paintings with my best friend—a different best friend, a second best friend. He had a gallery pass and he talks a lot—that's fine, I can assume the role of the listener, and sometimes I don't really care to assert an opinion, and my second best friend has plenty of 'em, so I listen as he talks about Claude Monet, and Monet's love of bridges: how Monet frames many of his paintings with a bridge, which introduces industrial scaled structure, it toys with scale and distance, and the solidity of the structure is still susceptible to the mutability of the light. My friend is so smart. And then I begin to talk about Monet's water lilies: "On the flat surface of the canvas he paints the water lilies, and he paints the reflection of the sky, and he paints the barely visible depths, the three dimensions are like past, present and future, all time mingling seamlessly on the flat surface of his canvas." And as I talk, I feel an odd sensation in my mouth. I poke it with the end of my tongue and a tooth dislodges. I reach in my mouth, I take it out…

Revealing tooth.

…and put it in my back pocket *(Does so.)* and without saying anything about the tooth to my second best friend I continue to talk about Claude Monet.

Monet must have meditated, he must have been able to feel a single water molecule dancing on the end of his nose. Somehow with Monet there is the mystery of the unseen, the figure lurking in the misty light, just behind it something fleeting, something lost. All is water, all is light, all is flow…

Returning to chair.

Don't worry, the end will come, gently, or it comes violently, each end arrives differently. But everything ends. Shows end, plagues end, lives end, and each end is a communion with the infinite unknown, and this torture of sitting, sitting with a shattering pain in my shoulder and a futile annoyance with Goinka, with my body and my failure and my limitations and there's nothing in all this, nothing in all that nothing, and we're nearing the end.

Tomorrow morning noble silence will be broken.

As the day winds down, Goinka tells us that every moment is precious, use every moment, but that just puts pressure on me, don't put pressure on me—and I'm arguing with Goinka again.

We can feel the end coming.

Bell and slide: "DAY 10"

Metappana. Goinka introduces us to metappana, the meditation on love for others. Metappana is the final meditation before we break noble silence.

"I pardon all those who have harmed me, either knowingly or unknowingly. May I be pardoned by all those I have harmed, either knowingly or unknowingly. May I be free of hatred, free of anger, free of ill will. May I generate love and goodwill. May all beings share my merits. May all beings share my peace, my harmony. May all beings be happy, be peaceful, be liberated... liberated... liberated."

Long pause.

Sometimes I feel I have not understood. I have been ignorant of the art of living, and I have always lived like this.

My shoulder hurts.

We leave the meditation hall, and noble silence is broken.

Light shift.

I don't feel like chatting.

Stands and places chair upstage right.

But noble silence is broken, and everyone is noble chatting, so I chat.

As he comes back centre:

And my first word is…

Light on audience.

Hello.

And all the characters who have shared my ten days of silence come to life.

Tony Small. He told me about his lively life in San Francisco, and how he moved back east to take care of his two dying parents, which he did, for five years, by himself. Now he's a bit of a shut-in, withdrawn from life. He had a tough retreat. Lots of confusion, unhappiness. I told him I had terminal cancer and there were many things I had to do to maintain my health in order to get through the ten days, many rules I had to break—which is partly a lie—it is a lie. I didn't have to break them, I wanted to and I did, and I told him it would have been distracting, for both of us. He didn't respond. I know, it's difficult to respond to that. I hope I didn't shame him. Tony Small. The puppy. He followed me around for the rest of the retreat. Sad. He was very sad. We're all a little sad.

The Bell Jar. From Guelph. He worked at the university there, I can't remember at what, his parents were psychoanalysts, he was between careers. He told me he played water polo passionately for fifteen years. An elbow clipped him in the head and gave him a bad concussion, it took him six months to recover and then… he was hit by a bus. He had headaches that got worse as the meditation proceeded. He told me that and more as he leaned against the bowed wood railing of the little footbridge, the brook babbling below. I didn't. Babble. About my cancer. I didn't hug him. I wished him luck, and moved on. We all move on.

Jason the Handsome is an environmentalist, he works in environmental safety. He's smart, he's liberal, he's perfectly bilingual and he's perfectly handsome. I had greater hopes for him. I thought he might also be naughty. He was there with his girlfriend. He was a little boring. I guess we're all a little boring.

The Dancer. He was actually an athlete. He was a professional soccer player. He felt something was missing in his life, and somehow found Vipassana.

We talked. He was the sweetest soul. And then his mother came to pick him up. She was very beautiful, from Trinidad, I kind of fell in love with her, so I wanted to give her something: I told her she had a beautiful son. I congratulated her, and thanked her for loving a fine human into the world. He was an athlete. But a dancer too. I could tell. I suspect that some of you are dancers.

And the Regurgitator, who swallowed his own vomit, he was so soft and unassertive, he was from India. I can't remember anything else about him. He was from India.

I loved India. I loved me in India. I loved Her.

And Fast Walker. Great guy. He builds YMCAs across the country. He told me, "I took you for a Bay Street type." Me? Really? That could be a little anti-Semitism, and it's the private school boy shining through, the UCC reserve, the white privilege. But I'll tell ya, eleven years as a little Jew boy at UCC was no privilege, more of a punishment. I suffered.

I did. But I learned. I learned the great privilege of being alive.

Oh. And François. Sweet François. We talked but I didn't understand a word he said. His French is very accented—Québécois. I'm only good at bourgeois Parisian French.

Isn't that amazing, that one day, my ship will sail into the horizon and my mediocre knowledge of French will disappear.

When my ship has sailed. When they lower the curtain. When I bite the dust. When I kick the bucket, cash in my chips, shuffle off and meet my maker. Boy, death is gonna be really busy.

My thoughts turn to the world, to which I will return, the world where not everyone has taken an ethical vow to abstain from killing, stealing, lying, the taking of intoxicants, and the fifth.

I pack my bags. I look for Tony Small to say goodbye. I can't find him.

Oh, last bit of cancer etiquette: if you outlive me, after I die, please don't say he valiantly fought cancer. I didn't fight cancer, it was not a battle, it was a love affair. I danced with cancer.

Music begins.

It's time to go.

It's just a body. My body and not my body.

Just a mind, mere mind, changing, changing, changing.

We all die. You will die, the time of your death is uncertain, so live well now, and be generous and—not that I mean to preach. There's no lesson here, I didn't want there to be a lesson—well that's a bit of a lesson *(Bit of panic, pressed by music.)* I'm not ready, I'm not fixed yet, I haven't worked out the ending yet, just one more day, one more day, I'm scared. I'm scared! *(Trying to calm.)* Okay. It's okay, it's only a feeling, observe the feeling, equanimity, equanimity, changing, changing, changing.

By now the words are barely audible, but we see his mouth move.

May all beings be happy, may all beings be peaceful, be liberated, liberated, liberated...

He is still. The music ends as the lights slowly fade to black.

Applause (likely).

Light gently comes up on audience.

The stage is empty.

Afterword

I'm still alive.

Obviously.

Today, July 20, 2022.

I finished performing *Other People* almost four months ago.

My health is unstable. I've been on a targeted therapy, Brigatinib, for almost eight months, but my left lung is inflamed and some of my lymph nodes are growing, and it seems, for the fourth time, that I will have to change treatments. As one uncouth fellow in my oncology clinic put it, "our options are dwindling." Likely, I'm heading for a second round of chemo.

I am caught in a terrible dilemma. I want to live, I want to thrive, there are still things to do. I realize, of course, there will always be things to do. Whenever my father had a health crisis which required an operation, a stop to his activities, he would lament "right in the middle of everything," as if there were anything that wasn't in the middle of everything. Which is to say, at some point, there won't be more for me to do because there won't be a me to do it. But for now there's still the hunger to write that thing, to go to Iceland, to walk in Gros Morne, just one more canoe trip, hang in there until a grandchild is born, to learn more about the prison abolition movement, to understand the origins of everything, more, more… let me catch my breath.

In the meantime, the future is uncertain (yes, as always, for everybody, the future is uncertain, yes yes yes) and I cannot make plans until I figure out what to do with my cancer treatment. Plus the sciatica, driving is excruciatingly painful. Plus the tendonitis in the shoulder, I can't paddle, plus the fatigue, plus I may start chemo next week so I can't make commitments, plus I'm tight with money so I don't want to lose a non-refundable deposit, plus at this point why do anything anyway, plus what's there to do, plus what's there to learn, plus I hate that bucket list bullshit, plus… calm down. I'll stop, and get to the point.

Performing *Other People* was demanding. Months before rehearsal began, I started to learn lines, some of which I knew would be rewritten. It required daily discipline and concentration. Rehearsal itself was stimulating and at times thrilling. I stayed focused for seven or eight hours a day, and the rest of my time, before and after rehearsal each day, was filled with self-care: feeding myself good food, doing tai chi, meditating, taking care of body and mind. And then the performance—weeks of people watching me, listening to me, giving me their attention, and me returning their attention with the full force of a spirit I tried to conjure each evening, a spirit of liberation and love. After the run of the show was done, I became a civilian again. Waking up in the mornings became difficult. I awoke without purpose, without energy, without knowing what to do with my day. I was saved for two weeks—I took my daughters to Paris—but after and since then, I have been seeking purpose, and fighting the looming prospect of another decline in health, another shift in treatment.

Now that I've done the show, announced my illness to the world, talked about dying, implied that this might be my last spring, I am concerned that I've had my say, and that's it. Any more out of me and people are bound to respond with "Is he still around, I thought he was dying, was all that just a ruse, when the hell is he going to die, enough already." At the same time, I want to engage, I want to learn, I want to be a part of the world. Will the United States turn into a dictatorship by a right-wing Christian nationalist minority? If so, how will people fight back? How will the liberal white middle class reconcile with the progressive movement that is making some sharp demands? How will the progressive movement reconcile with its own very difficult contradictions? What will happen to the weather?

What will happen to water? To the Toronto Maple Leafs? To my children? I am reading about the proposed abolition of the police and prison system, and I wonder why I am bothering—every generation has its thinking, new ideas, new pressures and new responses to those pressures, new language. Why bother to learn yet another language? It will just be replaced, eventually, by another response, another language. Perhaps the yearning for justice is deep and immortal. Perhaps I'm trying to understand it to stave off mortality: If I understand the new language about race and gender deep within me, if I engage with young minds, I'll survive into the next generation, it will extend my existence, somehow. It is a mystical thinking.

I also have a simple desire to belong, to continue to remain in relationship with others, as cancer and decline in health nudge me towards the inevitable aloneness of death.

These two forces, post-show, pull at me. One, an urge to live, an urge to belong, and the other a sobering feeling that I have played my cards and it's time to be quiet, plant some seeds on the balcony, go for walks, and sing songs, if necessary by myself.

Living post-performance is like living a new life, and having to reinvent myself is not easy, it never is, and aren't I fortunate that I have that opportunity—to have been someone, and to imagine that being someone else is still possible, even with the cancer in my body, even with the world on fire.

In the meantime, there are certain conventions that I would still like to observe—like acknowledging the people whose attention, advice, and generosity helped me produce *Other People.*

I'd like to acknowledge the tremendous legacy of S.A. Goinka, whose teaching is at the core of my meditation practice. In the play, I emphasize the restlessness of my mind while on retreat, and I appear to be quite critical of Goinka. In truth, I am deeply respectful of his work. The structure of the ten-day retreat is carefully rendered, and I think, quite exceptional. One thing follows another, beautifully layered and paced. The support on the retreat—all volunteer—is exceptional. Goinka also insisted that the participants not be charged a fee, that payment be purely on a donation basis. He did not want a transactional relationship. As he cheekily put it, "If meditators don't pay, they can't complain about the food." And the food, by the way, has at every retreat I have attended been tasty, healthy, and abundant. So thanks to Goinka, and all the other people who accompanied me on the Montebello retreat.

When young theatre makers have, in the past, asked me how to go about making a show, how do you start, what are the steps, I answer, "Book a venue." It sounds a bit flip, and it's advice that may not apply to all creative souls, but for me the words "Book a venue" are words to live by. Once the venue—the theatre, studio, it can be a living room—once it is booked, there is no turning back, and decisions must be made. Leonard Bernstein put it a different way when asked what it takes to make a great work of art: "Talent, and not enough time." Booking a venue seals the not-enough-time part of the equation by limiting your time, and the talent part can be achieved by finding talented collaborators.

I cannot speak for my own talent, but I can speak for the talent of the people I have involved in my work over the years, and on the play you hold in your hands.

I don't know who I spoke to first about wanting to create something out of my cancer experience, but it was likely Daniel MacIvor. He has been my creative partner over many decades. He understands and misunderstands me with equal passion, and cares about my work, sometimes more than I do. He offered advice at various points in the writing and was formally hired as "dramaturge" before we began our first workshop. He offered extremely useful advice, particularly regarding cuts that needed to be made, and in making those cuts we built the structure of the play.

The first person who I shared early writing with was Ravi Jain, who suggested the title "The Perfect Human." His initial interest and encouragement gave me momentum. He had momentum of his own on other projects, and I took the script in different directions, but his initial enthusiasm gave me life blood.

Brendan Healey was another talent that I reached out to, and I was fortunate to have him not only program the play at the theatre of which he is an artistic director, but to direct the play as well. He was enormously sensitive to my intentions, to what was "special" about the piece, always honest but sensitive in his criticism, full of useful and clarifying questions. Brendan is also a relentless searcher for what I would call an emotional narrative. Following our first run-through of the play, which occurred two weeks into rehearsal, a run-through that stank—I was too scared and too annoyed at my incompetence and the performance was tight and angry—his note session following the performance was passionate and concise. He went through the entire play, breaking it down into its relevant sections, pleading with me passionately, and articulating, with finesse, what was happening, what the play was saying, and he brought himself to tears, so engaged was he in the movement of my play. After he finished, MacIvor thanked him, and told him it was the best note session he had ever experienced. Which pissed me off—not only had I just delivered a shitty performance, but I had directed MacIvor a thousand times and given him ten thousand note sessions and Brendan Healey does one bloody note session and it's the best ever! But it was the best ever, and it guided me through the rest of rehearsal and the thirteen performances I did at Canadian Stage.

And by the way, I'm not going to tell you whether or not I sent him *Man's Search for Meaning.*

Among the other great talents who helped me was my dear friend Kristen Thompson. She was the first person I actually read the play to. Her questions, attention, and laughter were invaluable. My brother Adam and my third best friend Guillermo both read the play at various stages. Both were enormously encouraging and offered very useful advice.

There was abundant goodwill behind this project. Everyone wanted it, and me, to succeed. The circumstances demanded it.

Finally. I spent several months learning the text, and my first attempt at speaking it without reading was in a snowstorm at a cottage in Georgian Bay, to my fourth best friend Michael, who has brain cancer. His deep loving attention gave me strength.

The second attempt to speak the text without aid was over Zoom, with my daughter Kate. She had a few good suggestions for me. What a thrill to work on a creative project with my daughter, who, from the womb, entered the world into my waiting hands.

Her elder sister Emma decided that she did not want to read the play, but wanted to experience it for the first time in public performance. Imagine watching your father perform such a thing. Performing this show, opening night, with my daughters in the audience, my brother and dear sister-in-law, their two children, Daniel, Brendan (in spirit—he was home with Covid), Thomas, Kim P., Arwen, Adam L., Leah, Don, Patricia, Chad, Joe, Kristen, Frank, John, Pamela, Rob, Marilyn and other dear friends… an overwhelming experience. I could write a play about that performance alone. But I won't. I'm busy with other things. I'm learning about the ideas behind the prison abolition movement. And hoping that my friends and community will forgive me for living another year or two or three or….

Daniel Brooks

Daniel Brooks is one of Canada's most accomplished theatre makers. As a writer, director, and performer, he has collaborated with some of the country's finest talents in producing a body of daring and original work. He has created shows with Don McKellar, Tracy Wright, Daniel MacIvor, Guillermo Verdecchia, John Mighton, and Michael Ondaatje, among others. His many achievements include a series of monologues created with Daniel MacIvor, direction of work by John Mighton, Beckett, Chekhov, Ibsen, Sophocles, Borges, and Goethe, as well as the musical *Drowsy Chaperone.* His published work includes *Insomnia, The Noam Chomsky Lectures, The Eco Show, The Good Life, Bigger Than Jesus,* and *The Full Light of Day.* He was co-artistic director of the Augusta Company, and artistic director of Necessary Angel from 2003 to 2012. He was also a playwright-in-residence at the Tarragon Theatre for seven years and the Barker Fairley Distinguished Visitor at the University of Toronto. His many theatre awards include the Siminovitch Prize in Theatre. His work has toured across Canada and around the world.